Contents

Some words are shown in bold, **like this**. You can find out what they mean by looking in the glossary.

Why does history matter?

Do you ever wonder why we learn history? History is more than just amazing stories from the past. When we study history, we learn why the world is the way it is today. We can also learn from mistakes people made in the past.

Animals that lived in the past are a part of history.

Some people like to remember history by acting it out again.

History can be very exciting. Many people like to learn about history all their lives. Read this book to find out about some great jobs that involve history. Could one of them be for you?

Be a museum curator

If you like finding out about objects from the past then maybe you could be a museum curator. Your job would be to get new **artefacts** for a museum. Sometimes you might swap artefacts with other museums.

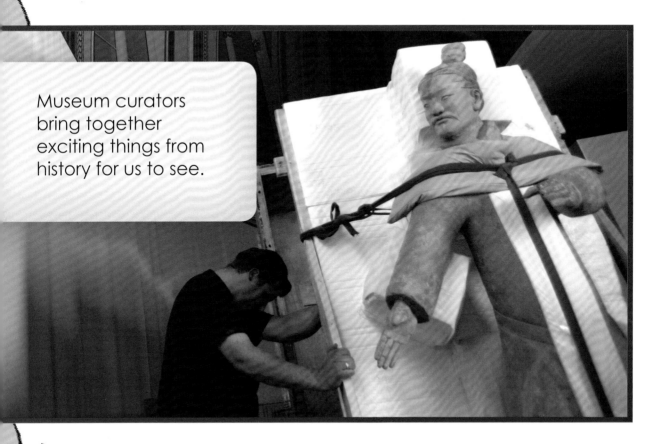

Museum curators bring together exciting things from history for us to see.

Museum curators know how to handle very old objects properly.

Museum curators have to organize all the objects in their museum so visitors can understand them. They need to make sure the artefacts are looked after carefully. Sometimes they might talk to people about the objects in the museum.

Be an archaeologist

If you were an archaeologist, you would look for places where objects from history might be found. Then you would work with a team on an **excavation**. You would carefully dig up the ground and look for **artefacts** from history.

These archaeologists are digging up the remains of a pyramid in Egypt.

When archaeologists find artefacts, they clean and identify them. Sometimes they do tests in a **laboratory** to find out how old an artefact is. They might use computers to show how a place looked hundreds of years ago.

This archaeologist is looking closely at an artefact to find out more about it.

Be a conservator

If you were a conservator, your job would be to look after art and objects from history. You would probably **specialize** in one type of object, such as sculpture, costumes, or paintings. You would work in a **laboratory** as well as visit museums and **art galleries**.

A conservator knows how to clean a painting without damaging it.

Conservators know how to handle artefacts with care.

Conservators look at objects carefully to see if they are damaged. They make repairs and **preserve** objects to keep them in a good condition. They make sure **artefacts** are kept in a safe place where they won't be damaged.

Be a costume designer

If you love clothes and history then maybe you could be a costume designer! When people set plays, television programmes, or films in the past, they need the right costumes. A costume designer designs and makes clothes from history.

Costume designers know how clothes from history should look.

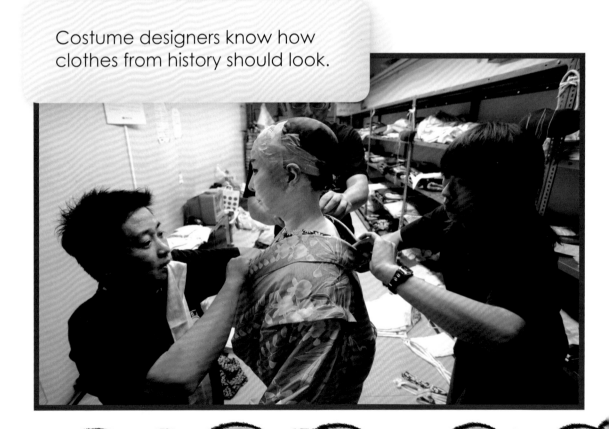

Costume designers draw their ideas after doing research.

Costume designers read the **script**, then **research** the clothes people wore at that time in history. Then they sketch their ideas and talk to the other people working on the play or film. When everyone is happy they make the clothes.

e a teacher

If you really love history then a great job for you could be teaching. You would teach children about the world and how it has changed over time. You would help children to see how the past helps us to make decisions about the future.

Sometimes history teachers take their classes on trips.

Primary school teachers tell children how history fits in with everything else they learn at school. At secondary school some teachers **specialize** in history. Teachers sometimes organize trips to museums and other places to find out more about the past.

History teachers can take children on lots of fun trips!

e a researcher

If you were a researcher, it would be your job to find information and share it with people. You might do **research** for a television or radio programme or for a company report. You would need to find the facts and check they were correct.

Researchers might look at old film to find out about the past.

Researchers sometimes use very old books to do their work.

Researchers use libraries, museums, and the Internet to find information. Often, they have to find out about life in the past. Knowing about history helps them to find the facts they need and to write about this information in a clear way.

Be an archivist

If you like reading as well as history then maybe you could be an archivist. An archivist looks after important **records** and documents from history. Some archivists take care of old books or maps, while others look after photographs, film, or sound files.

Archivists wear gloves to stop them damaging old books.

Archivists organize collections so they can find documents easily.

Archivists make sure that collections are kept in a safe place. They organize the documents in the archive and help people to look at them. Sometimes archivists put the documents in their collection on the Internet so many people can look at them.

Be a museum educator

If you were a museum educator, your job would be to talk to museum visitors. You would help people to understand history by talking about it. You would also show them objects and explain what they were used for in the past.

Museum educators help to bring history to life.

Some museum educators organize activities for children visiting a museum or **art gallery**. These activities help children to understand **exhibitions**. They might help children to handle objects in the museum's collection.

Museum educators help visitors understand what life was like in the past.

Be an auctioneer

If you were an **auctioneer**, you would look at **antiques** people wanted to sell. You would check the objects to see if they were in good condition. Then you would decide how much the objects could sell for.

Auctioneers need to know a lot about objects from history.

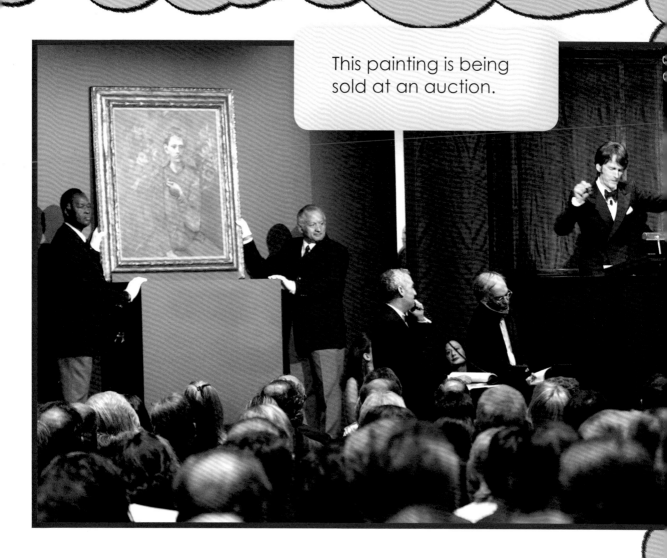

This painting is being sold at an auction.

Auctioneers give information to people who are thinking about buying an object. They hold an auction, where people can offer to buy the object. The person who offers the highest price gets the object.

Be a tour guide

If you were a tour guide, you might show people around a place or area that has an important history. Some tour guides show visitors around old buildings. Other tour guides take people around a city and tell them what happened there in the past.

A tour guide can show people the important places in a city.

Tour guides need to remember a lot of facts from history. They need to be good at talking to people about the past in an interesting way. They need to know a lot of information to answer people's questions.

Tour guides tell people interesting facts and stories.

Choosing the right job for you

When you decide what you want to do when you grow up, don't just think about school subjects. Think about what you enjoy doing. If you like talking to people then you could be a museum educator or tour guide.

If you're interested in clothes and art then you could be a costume designer. There are so many exciting jobs using history that there is something to suit everyone.

Five things you couldn't do without history

- Be a good citizen
- Understand where your family and friends come from
- Learn from mistakes people made in the past
- Enjoy amazing stories about people in the past
- Understand why your world works the way it does

History job chart

If you want to find out more about any of the jobs in this book, start here:

	Archaeologist	Archivist	Auctioneer	Conservator	
You need to:	Be very careful and patient	Be careful and organized	Know what different **antiques** are worth	Know a lot about objects from history	
Best thing about it:	Discovering old and unusual objects!	Working with very old documents that not many people see!	Selling antiques for a big price!	Sharing amazing **artefacts** with many people!	

Costume designer	Museum curator	Museum educator	Researcher	Teacher	Tour guide
Be interested in fashion	Know a lot about historical objects	Be good at explaining history to people	Be good at finding information	Enjoy helping people to learn	Know a lot of information about a place
Seeing your costumes on the screen!	Seeing visitors enjoy your **exhibitions**!	Having fun sharing history with visitors!	Finding incredible facts about the past!	Seeing your pupils get excited about history!	Bringing history to life for people!

Glossary

antique object made a long time ago

auctioneer person who sells things at auctions

art gallery place where paintings and sculptures are displayed

artefact object made by people

excavation digging up of objects from history

exhibition place where pieces of art and artefacts are displayed for people to look at

laboratory place where research can be done on objects from the past

preserve keep something safe from damage

record written information

research find as much information about something as possible

script words that are spoken in a play, film, or television programme

specialize focus on one particular area

Find out more

The Young Archaeologists' Club
www.britarch.ac.uk/yac/
This website will help you to find out more
about archaeology.

The British Museum
www.britishmuseum.org/explore/young_explorers1.
aspx
Discover more about history and the artefacts at
the British Museum on this website.

Museum of Costume
www.museumofcostume.co.uk/htmlContent/
game.html
Play a game on this website to find out more about
costumes from the past.

Index